THE 2011 STAMP YEARBOOK

UNITED STATES POSTAL SERVICE

The designs of stamps and postal stationery are the subject of
individual copyrights by the United States Postal Service. UNITED
STATES POSTAL SERVICE, the eagle logo, and POSTAL SERVICE
are trademarks of the United States Postal Service.

Stamp art © U.S. Postal Service

Design and production by Journey Group, Inc.

ISBN 978-0-9796569-4-1

Enhance your *2011 Stamp Yearbook* by ordering the mail use stamps
featured in the second part of this book. For just $22.50, you'll get
43 stamps and their corresponding mounts. To order item # 991104
while supplies last, call 1 800 STAMP-24.

Other books available from the United States Postal Service:
The 2010 Stamp Yearbook
The Postal Service Guide to U.S. Stamps, 38th Edition

THE 2011 STAMP YEARBOOK

UNITED STATES POSTAL SERVICE

UNITED STATES
POSTAL SERVICE ®

CONTENTS

FROM HERE TO FOREVER

STAMPS HIGHLIGHT A SLICE OF AMERICAN LIFE AND FREEZE IT FOREVER IN TIME.

In 2011, they also serve as milestones: This year, for the first time, the U.S. Postal Service issued all First-Class commemoratives as Forever® stamps.

We know that stamps are the main reason you visit Post Offices and a vital reason you keep coming back. By issuing our most stunning commemoratives as Forever stamps, we hope you'll more easily find your favorites—whether at Post Offices, through *usps.com,* or wherever stamps are sold. Now you'll be able to collect them or use them for mailing as long as you like, even when the rate changes.

Throughout 2011, stamps proclaimed their nationwide reach. In Austin, Texas, South by Southwest concertgoers cheered the Latin Music Legends stamps, while theater buffs in Washington, D.C., enjoyed the dedication of the Helen Hayes stamp at the awards show named for the actress herself. At historic Kennedy Space Center in Florida, we launched stamps to celebrate half a century of American space exploration. In Charleston, South Carolina, we solemnly gathered to issue the first of several stamps to mark the sesquicentennial of the Civil War.

From coast to coast, the public embraces the beauty and diversity of stamps. We meet numerous longtime collectors, but we also talk to newcomers who simply adore a recent issuance. We love stamps, too, so our goal is simple: to keep the public excited about them so that each new issuance continues to honor our nation's best—this year, next year, and forever.

STEPHEN M. KEARNEY
Executive Director, Stamp Services
U.S. Postal Service

After he toured the United States in the 1830s, French political philosopher and historian Alexis de Tocqueville was fascinated to discover that Americans saw their roles in their young nation partly in terms of "the recollections of the past, the labors of the present, and the hopes of the future." The collectible stamps on these pages attest to the persistence of American vision, an awareness that the better we understand the heroism and heartbreak that came before us, the more clearly we see ourselves.

> PART

1

COLLECT
STAMPS

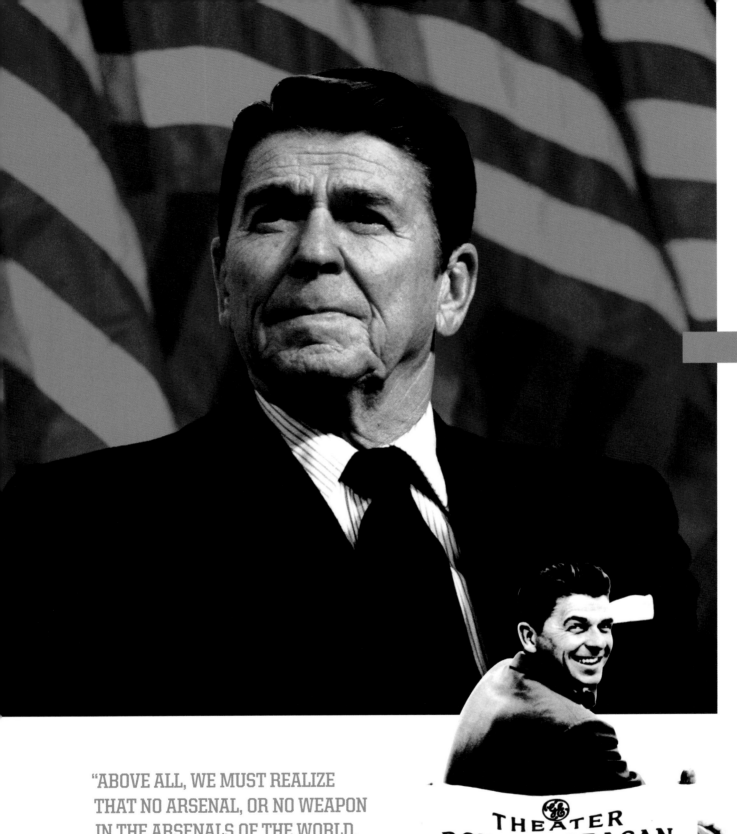

"ABOVE ALL, WE MUST REALIZE
THAT NO ARSENAL, OR NO WEAPON
IN THE ARSENALS OF THE WORLD,
IS SO FORMIDABLE AS THE WILL
AND MORAL COURAGE OF FREE
MEN AND WOMEN."

— first inaugural address, January 20, 1981

RONALD REAGAN CENTENNIAL

> HISTORY

A Hollywood actor who appeared in more than 50 films before becoming a prominent political leader, Ronald Wilson Reagan (1911–2004) was known as the "Great Communicator." He is often credited with bolstering the conservative movement in America, moving it from the margins of politics to the mainstream.

In 1937, after a successful career as a radio sports announcer in the Midwest, Ronald Reagan went to California and landed a movie contract with Warner Bros. During World War II, he produced and narrated training films, and he twice served as president of the Screen Actors Guild.

In 1964, Ronald Reagan gave a nationally televised address endorsing Republican presidential candidate Barry Goldwater. Although Goldwater lost the election, Ronald Reagan's speech—a searing indictment against big government and Johnson's "Great Society" programs—effectively launched his own political career. Two years later, he defeated the incumbent governor of California by a landslide. In 1970, he was elected to a second term.

Pledging to reduce the size and influence of the federal government and to make Americans believe in themselves again, Ronald Reagan ran for president in 1980 and won a landslide victory over incumbent president Jimmy Carter.

On January 20, 1981, he was sworn into office as the 40th President of the United States.

As president, he persuaded Congress to pass legislation aimed at curbing inflation, increasing employment, reducing social welfare programs, and strengthening national defense. "Peace through Strength" is how President Reagan characterized his foreign policy toward the Soviet Union. Shortly after Mikhail Gorbachev came to power in the Soviet Union, the two leaders met in Geneva in 1985 and committed themselves to arms reduction and to improving relations between their countries.

When President Reagan left office in January 1989, he and former First Lady Nancy Reagan returned to California. Later that year, on November 9, Communist East Germany opened its borders—including the Berlin Wall—to the West. This momentous event occurred less than two and a half years after President Reagan's famous speech at the Brandenburg Gate, in which he had boldly challenged Gorbachev to "tear down this wall!"

This stamp is one of a number of centennial events taking place in 2011 to commemorate President Reagan's life and legacy. The artwork was based on a photograph of Ronald Reagan taken at his beloved California ranch during his second presidential term.

INDIANAPOLIS 500®

In 1909, an investment team led by entrepreneur and automobile dealer Carl Graham Fisher purchased 320 acres of farmland outside Indianapolis, Indiana, with the intention of creating a speedway for both racing competitions and private testing. After a series of motorcycle and automotive races, Fisher decided to focus on a single event: an ambitious 500-mile race to be held on Memorial Day.

On May 30, 1911, the Indianapolis Motor Speedway hosted the first Indianapolis 500. Around 80,000 spectators watched Ray Harroun beat 39 other drivers with a time of 6 hours, 42 minutes, and 8 seconds in a car manufactured by the Indianapolis-based Marmon Motor Car Company and nicknamed the "Wasp" for its yellow paint and long, aerodynamic tail. Harroun, who designed the car, included his own invention: the rearview mirror.

In 1927, the founders sold the Speedway to a group led by World War I flying ace and fellow entrepreneur Captain Eddie Rickenbacker. The decades that followed brought the financial hardships of the Great Depression, and World War II forced the closing of the track.

In 1945, Rickenbacker sold the dilapidated Speedway to Indiana entrepreneur Tony Hulman. Beginning with the Indy 500 on Memorial Day weekend in 1946, Hulman revived the Indianapolis Motor Speedway and oversaw the Indianapolis 500 until his death in 1977. Today, the Speedway remains in the Hulman family, and the Indy 500, billed as "The Greatest Spectacle in Racing," has become one of the most significant auto races in the world.

33 CARS

2.5 MILES PER LAP

MORE THAN 250,000 SPECTATORS

A CENTURY OF HISTORY

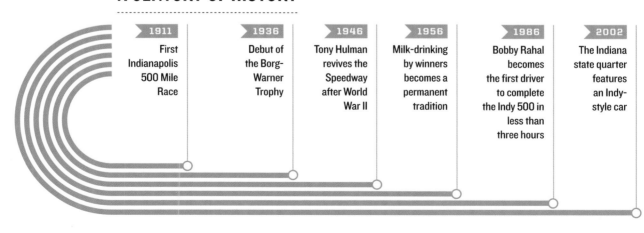

1911
First Indianapolis 500 Mile Race

1936
Debut of the Borg-Warner Trophy

1946
Tony Hulman revives the Speedway after World War II

1956
Milk-drinking by winners becomes a permanent tradition

1986
Bobby Rahal becomes the first driver to complete the Indy 500 in less than three hours

2002
The Indiana state quarter features an Indy-style car

LATIN MUSIC LEGENDS

CARLOS GARDEL Known as "the man with the tear in his voice," Carlos Gardel (1890?–1935) had a superb baritone voice tailor-made for the tango. His charm, dapper attire, and magnetic stage presence excited audiences in Latin America, Spain, and Paris, as well as in movie houses, where he achieved fame as one of the stars of Spanish-language cinema. In the U.S., Gardel sang for NBC Radio, made a number of Spanish-language movies, and had just completed work on his first film for the English-speaking market when his life was cut short in an airplane accident. Through ten sound films and hundreds of recordings, Gardel became one of the most popular tango artists of all time.

CELIA CRUZ A dazzling performer of many genres of Afro-Caribbean music, Celia Cruz (1925–2003) had a powerful contralto voice, energetic stage presence, and a unique style that endeared her to fans from different nationalities and across generations. One of few women to succeed in the male-dominated world of salsa music, the "Queen of Salsa" performed for more than five decades and recorded more than 50 albums. Skilled in the art of improvisational singing, Cruz chose a repertoire that showcased her command of complex rhythms and melodies. Dressed in fantastic gowns and elaborate wigs, she would cry "*¡Azúcar!*" ("Sugar!" in Spanish) to evoke associations with Cuban culture and energize her audiences. Cruz continually reinvented herself, collaborating with non-salsa musicians and demonstrating her versatility in dramatic film and television roles.

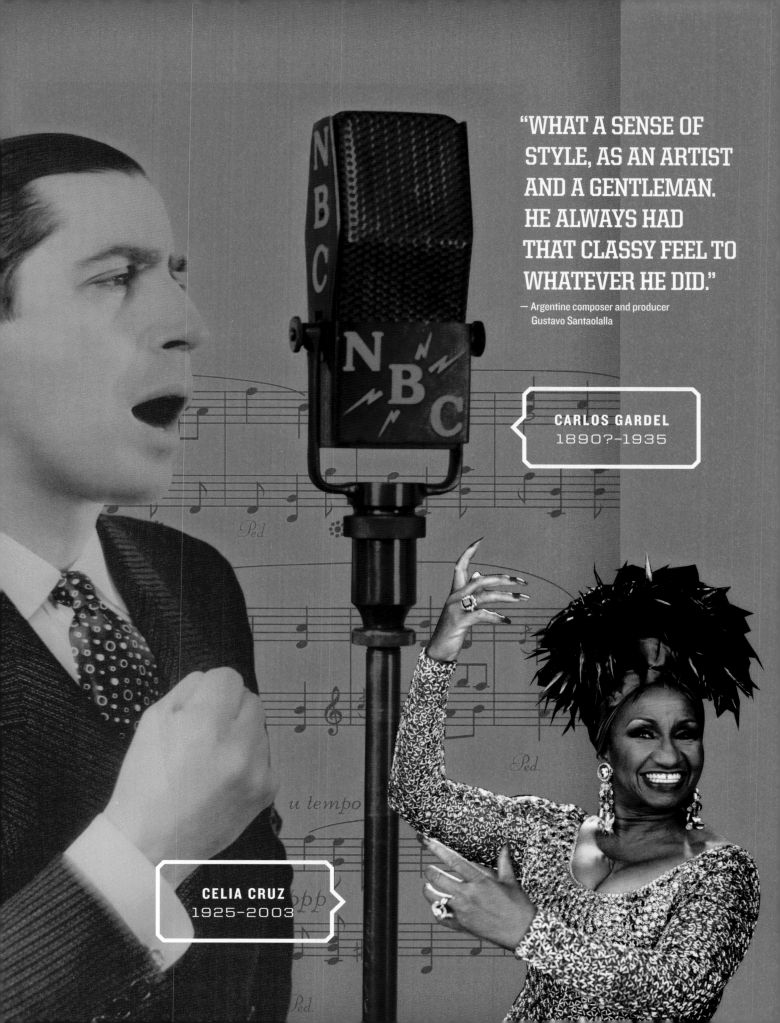

"WHAT A SENSE OF STYLE, AS AN ARTIST AND A GENTLEMAN. HE ALWAYS HAD THAT CLASSY FEEL TO WHATEVER HE DID."
— Argentine composer and producer Gustavo Santaolalla

CARLOS GARDEL
1890?-1935

CELIA CRUZ
1925-2003

SELENA A charismatic entertainer with a rich and emotional vocal style, Selena Quintanilla-Perez (1971–1995)—known to fans simply as Selena—helped transform and popularize Tejano, a combination of Mexican *ranchera*-style music mixed with German polka sounds, by integrating it with techno–hip-hop beats, disco-influenced dance movements, and a captivating stage presence. Remembered for her warm and ebullient personality, strong voice, sparkling wardrobe, and a stage presence described as simultaneously sexy and wholesome, Selena was an important representative of Latino culture in America. Her legacy as the "Queen of Tejano" expanded after her tragic death, when millions more Americans were introduced to her earlier recordings.

CARMEN MIRANDA Captivating audiences with her Latin charm, Carmen Miranda (1909–1955) enjoyed a remarkable film, stage, and radio career. Best known for her interpretation of the Brazilian samba, she further distinguished herself on nightclub stages by amusing and playing with her audiences. Mischievous, coquettish, and provocative, the "Brazilian Bombshell" appeared in 14 Hollywood musicals and recorded more than 300 songs. Today her name, image, and vocal style live on in homages and impersonations in film and on television, as countless people continue to take pleasure in dressing up and projecting the joie de vivre that was her trademark.

TITO PUENTE A musical virtuoso as a performer, arranger, composer, and conductor, Tito Puente (1923–2000) was popularly known as *El Rey*, "The King." He helped build the bridge between Afro-Caribbean music and jazz with his passion for integrating traditional music with innovation. While his solos on the timbales and his percussive orchestrations are legendary, Puente also recorded more than 140 albums that feature a rich legacy of arrangements and compositions. *The New York Times* hailed his 1958 album *Dance Mania* as one of the most significant albums of the 20th century, and his many awards and honors included eight Grammys, the National Medal of the Arts, and the National Academy of Recording Arts and Sciences' Lifetime Achievement Award. He was also acknowledged as a Living Legend by the Library of Congress.

"EVERYTHING, THE APPLAUSE, THE FANS ASKING FOR AUTOGRAPHS, THE TRIPS, ALL THAT IS A DREAM."
— Selena

> **SELENA**
> 1971–1995

KANSAS STATEHOOD

Much of the land that now comprises Kansas first became part of the United States in 1803 following the Louisiana Purchase, when President Thomas Jefferson effectively doubled the size of the nation by overseeing the acquisition of more than 800,000 square miles of land from France. After the passage of the Kansas-Nebraska Act in 1854, settlers established governments in the two new territories, and Kansas became a battleground in the national debate over slavery. Pro-slavery and anti-slavery factions founded towns and developed competing legislatures and constitutions, and they often clashed violently. The raids of abolitionist John Brown and several significant battles and attacks prompted newspapers around the country to refer to the territory as "Bleeding Kansas."

In October 1857, the Free Staters won their first major victory in a recognized election, electing a Free State legislature and a Free State delegate to Congress. Because of the U.S. Supreme Court's decision in *Dred Scott v. Sandford* earlier that year, slavery was legal in Kansas as long as it remained a territory. After four constitutional conventions, the state constitution drafted in 1859 declared that slavery would not be legal in Kansas. When Kansas joined the Union on January 29, 1861, the issue of slavery was settled within the state's borders, although the start of the Civil War was less than three months away. As William Allen White, the renowned editor of the *Emporia Gazette,* would quip in 1922, "When anything is going to happen in this country, it happens first in Kansas."

"THEY HUNGER FOR THE HORIZON... BUT NO GENUINE KANSAN CAN EMIGRATE. HE MAY WANDER. HE MAY ROAM. HE MAY TRAVEL. HE MAY GO ELSEWHERE, BUT NO OTHER STATE CAN CLAIM HIM AS A CITIZEN. ONCE NATURALIZED, THE ALLEGIANCE CAN NEVER BE FORSWORN."

— Senator John James Ingalls (1833–1900)

KANSAS: THE 34ᵀᴴ STATE

STATEHOOD DATE
January 29, 1861

STATE MOTTO
Ad astra per aspera ("Through difficulties, to the stars")

STATE NICKNAME
The Sunflower State

FAMOUS KANSANS
Amelia Earhart, Langston Hughes, Charlie Parker, President Dwight D. Eisenhower

CURRENT POPULATION
approximately 2.8 million

MAJOR INDUSTRIES
Manufacturing, especially of aircraft and transportation equipment; agriculture; food production; mining; natural gas production

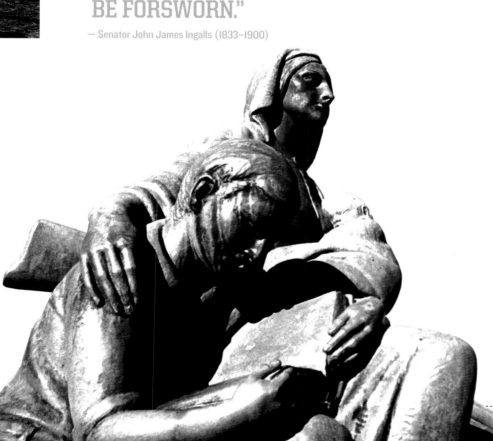

Depicting a tireless matriarch guarding her children, the Pioneer Mother Memorial was sculpted by Topeka-born Robert Merrell Gage (1892–1981). Dedicated in 1937, the monument stands on the grounds of the Kansas State Capitol not far from another of Gage's works, a much-praised statue of a seated Abraham Lincoln.

FIRST BULL RUN

"THE LAST RAY OF HOPE FOR PRESERVING THE UNION PEACEABLY EXPIRED AT THE ASSAULT UPON FORT SUMTER ..."

— Abraham Lincoln, 1861 State of the Union Address

FORT SUMTER

THE CIVIL WAR: 1861

> HISTORY

MAJOR
ROBERT ANDERSON

FORT SUMTER When Abraham Lincoln ran for president in 1860, his views on slavery were considered incendiary in the South. Slavery, said Lincoln, was a "monstrous injustice" that deprived America's republican example "of its just influence in the world." The nation could not remain half slave and half free; it would "become *all* one thing, or *all* the other."

South Carolina acted swiftly in response to Lincoln's election. On December 20, 1860, it became the first state to secede, precipitating a national crisis over Fort Sumter, a federal garrison at Charleston. The fort was under the command of Kentucky-born Robert Anderson, who was both devoted to the Union and sympathetic to the South.

With his troops at Fort Moultrie facing a growing threat from South Carolina militiamen, Anderson secretly moved them to Fort Sumter. While Anderson hoped to avoid bloodshed, his action provoked South Carolina to demand he surrender the fort, a vital symbol of independence to the South and national sovereignty to the North.

On his first full day in office in March 1861, President Lincoln learned that Fort Sumter was running short of provisions. He faced a stark choice: evacuate the fort and appear to acknowledge the Confederacy's independence, or send ships to Charleston and provoke war.

Winfield Scott, commanding general of the U.S. Army, saw no alternative to surrender, and most of the Cabinet likewise urged evacuation—but Lincoln looked for another option. He decided to send unarmed boats carrying, in his words, "food for hungry men." If Confederates fired on the boats, the South would be seen as the aggressor; if the supplies were allowed to go through, the Union would win an important symbolic victory in the court of public opinion.

After Lincoln announced his plan, Confederate President Jefferson Davis ordered General Pierre G. T. Beauregard to take Fort Sumter. On the morning of April 12, Confederates began shelling the fort, prompting Anderson's surrender a day and a half later.

On April 15, Lincoln called for 75,000 militiamen to serve for 90 days to put down the rebellion. The Civil War had begun.

FIRST BULL RUN

The Battle of First Bull Run—or Manassas, as Southerners called it—took place on July 21 some 30 miles southwest of Washington, D.C., near a stream called Bull Run, close to a vital rail line. By engaging Confederate forces there, Union forces hoped to avenge Fort Sumter and move on to Richmond, the Confederate capital.

On the march from Washington on July 16, the army of Union General Irvin McDowell, some 35,000 strong compared to Pierre Beauregard's 22,000 or so, advanced more slowly than expected, allowing time for Beauregard to concentrate his forces behind the protective barrier of Bull Run.

Soon after midnight on the day of the battle, McDowell's forces hoped to cross Bull Run early and catch the Confederates off guard, but the men moved slowly through the dark along narrow roads and fell behind schedule. By 9:30 A.M., when they finally began the crossing, the Confederates had repositioned some of their forces.

McDowell's men outnumbered the Confederates and seemed on the verge of a major victory by midday after pushing them up the slopes of Henry House Hill. During a lull in the battle, Brigadier General Thomas J. Jackson positioned regiments and artillery nearby and later acquired the nickname "Stonewall," reportedly by remaining firm before the Union onslaught and rallying his Virginia division. The tide turned when Confederate General Joseph E. Johnston arrived with 11,000 more soldiers. McDowell ordered his exhausted and dispirited volunteers back to Washington, ending the battle at Bull Run with a decisive Confederate victory.

Southerners hoped their victory might dissuade the North, but Lincoln prepared for a long war. The day after the battle, he signed a bill enlisting half a million three-year volunteers and summoned General George B. McClellan to command the new Army of the Potomac.

Approximately 900 soldiers died at First Bull Run and another 2,700 were wounded. While such casualties would pale in comparison to later battles, the death toll was shocking. According to historian David Detzer, "There had never been a day like it in the history of the nation."

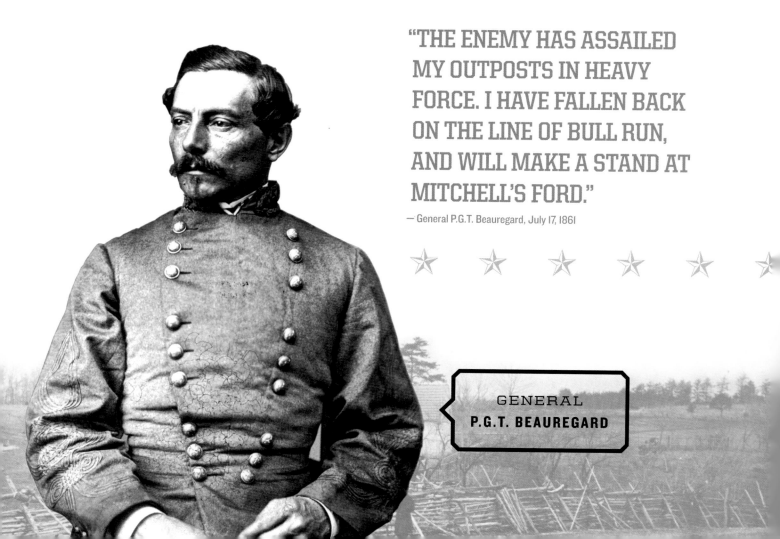

"THE ENEMY HAS ASSAILED MY OUTPOSTS IN HEAVY FORCE. I HAVE FALLEN BACK ON THE LINE OF BULL RUN, AND WILL MAKE A STAND AT MITCHELL'S FORD."

— General P.G.T. Beauregard, July 17, 1861

GENERAL
P.G.T. BEAUREGARD

THE CIVIL WAR
1861
A Nation Touched with Fire

The American people and the Government at Washington may refuse to recognize it for a time; but the "inexorable logic of events" will force it upon them in the end; that the war now being waged in this land is a war for and against slavery.

Frederick Douglass

I'll trace these gardens o'er and o'er,
Meditate on each sweet flower,
Thinking of each happy hour,
Oh, Johnny is gone for a soldier.

Traditional lament

The last ray of hope for preserving the Union peaceably expired at the assault upon Fort Sumter.

Abraham Lincoln

Fort Sumter April 12-13, 1861

I foresee that the country will have to pass through a terrible ordeal, a necessary expiation, perhaps, of our national sins.

Robert E. Lee

First Bull Run July 21, 1861

People who are anxious to bring on war don't know what they are bargaining for; they don't see all the horrors that must accompany such an event.

Thomas J. Jackson

"EVERYBODY STARTS AT THE TOP, AND THEN HAS THE PROBLEM OF STAYING THERE. LASTING ACCOMPLISHMENT, HOWEVER, IS STILL ACHIEVED THROUGH A LONG, SLOW CLIMB AND SELF-DISCIPLINE."

— Helen Hayes, *On Reflection: An Autobiography*

HELEN HAYES

H elen Hayes (1900–1993) was a radiant presence on Broadway for much of the 20th century. Born in Washington, D.C., she began acting at age 5 in a school production of Shakespeare's *A Midsummer Night's Dream* and developed into a promising child actress, soon establishing her persona as a happy, innocent, plucky type during a cross-country tour in the title role of *Pollyanna.*

When Hayes received her first star billing on Broadway at age 20 in the comedy *Bab,* audiences responded to her charm, grace, and honesty. In 1927, she began a three-year run on Broadway and on tour as the ill-fated heroine of *Coquette,* drawing praise as one of the country's best young players in serious drama as well as comedy.

Hayes capitalized on her growing success by launching a radio career in 1928 and a film career in 1931, while continuing to perform nearly every season on stage. She won an Academy Award for Best Actress for her talking-picture debut, *The Sin of Madelon Claudet* (1931). The following year, she played opposite Gary Cooper in the acclaimed film adaptation of *A Farewell to Arms.*

Subsequent notable stage performances, in New York and elsewhere, included *Happy Birthday* (1946), for which Hayes won the inaugural Tony Award for Outstanding Performance by an Actress; *Time Remembered* (1957), for which she won her second Tony Award; and Eugene O'Neill's *A Touch of the Poet* (1958). Altogether, Hayes appeared in more than 100 stage productions during the long span of her career, justly deserving the title "First Lady of the American Theater." When she died on March 17, 1993, at age 92, the lights of Broadway were dimmed in her honor.

In two of her most celebrated roles on Broadway, Hayes portrayed famous monarchs. Despite standing only five feet tall, she convincingly played Mary Stuart, one of history's tallest queens, in *Mary of Scotland* (1933). When she portrayed Queen Victoria from youth to old age in *Victoria Regina* (1935), Hayes revealed the full range of her talents. *Victoria Regina* ran for several years and nearly a thousand performances. "When you transcend yourself and really get inside the character," Hayes later wrote, "it's like being touched by God."

SEND A HELLO

Since 1986, Disney•Pixar films have stretched the boundaries of our imagination with stories about unlikely heroes who explore the bonds of friendship and family. Now some of those heroes are the subjects of colorful new stamps that encourage people to connect with loved ones through the mail.

Pixar Animation Studios, which celebrates its 25th anniversary in 2011, has earned 29 Academy Awards and seven Golden Globes, and its 12 feature films have grossed more than $6.5 billion worldwide at the box office. At the 66th Venice International Film Festival, Pixar directors John Lasseter, Andrew Stanton, Pete Docter, Brad Bird, and Lee Unkrich were honored with the Golden Lion for Lifetime Achievement. In their 12 feature films to date, these Pixar storytellers have consistently sent their own "hello" to the world, affirming the power of dreams and the importance of sharing them.

TOY STORY // 1995 *Toy Story*, the world's first full-length computer-animated film, took moviemaking to a new technological and artistic level. Featuring a pull-string cowboy named Woody, a space ranger action figure named Buzz Lightyear, and a host of out-of-the-toybox characters, *Toy Story* captured the imagination of audiences around the world.

CARS // 2006 *Cars* tells the story of Lightning McQueen, a fast-tracking racecar whose outlook on life gets a tune-up when he takes an unplanned detour in Radiator Springs, a sleepy little town along Route 66. Befriended by Mater, a rusty old tow truck with an engine of gold, Lightning learns the value of friendship—and hits the road to true success.

RATATOUILLE // 2007 Remy is a rat who dreams of becoming a great chef, but it takes help from the ghost of his culinary hero Auguste Gusteau and an awkward young man named Linguini to make his dreams come true.

WALL·E // 2008 The last little robot on Earth discovers a new purpose in life—as well as the key to Earth's future—when he falls for a sleek modern robot named EVE. Without saying a word, WALL·E's sound effects and movements convey the emotional range of any human performer.

UP // 2009 At 78, curmudgeonly former balloon salesman Carl Fredericksen finally fulfills his lifelong dream: He ties thousands of balloons to his house to fly away to the wilds of South America. When he finds himself on a great adventure with an overly-enthusiastic eight-year-old named Russell, a talking dog named Dug, and a 13-foot-tall rare flightless bird, he discovers that life's true adventure can be found not in travel or great accomplishments, but in small, everyday moments with family and friends.

GO GREEN

Sometimes it seems as if there isn't much we can do as individuals to help the environment. Fortunately, each of us can make a difference, as this stamp pane will attest. Playful but purposeful, the Go Green stamps illustrate simple changes we can make, showing that small steps can lead to big results—and a cleaner world for us all.

Most of us know that if we recycle cans and bottles, we reduce landfill waste, but the benefits don't end there. Making containers such as aluminum cans from raw rather than recycled materials is extremely energy-intensive and produces large amounts of carbon dioxide, so a year's worth of recycling saves energy equivalent to billions of gallons of gasoline. Recycling also reduces greenhouse gas emissions; it's as if we'd removed millions of cars from the roads.

You can "go green" under your own roof, too. Homes consume about one-fifth of all energy used in the United States—more than cars or planes—and around one-third of that energy is wasted when it escapes through cracks and poorly sealed areas. Even the simplest insulation, like caulking or weatherstripping, can be hugely beneficial to the environment—while reducing your utility bills as well.

These days, Americans are learning that our actions, both individually and collectively, affect the very air we breathe. Fortunately, this stamp pane sends an inspiring message: When we find ways to reduce waste and conserve natural resources, we all breathe a little easier.

PITCHING IN

Here at the Postal Service, we're doing our part. We're the only mailing and shipping company in the world whose packaging and postage products are certified as safe for human health and the environment. To cut emissions 20 percent by 2020, we're conserving energy at thousands of facilities and finding ways to use less petroleum fuel and water. Committed to reducing landfill waste, we also recycled more than 222,000 tons of material in 2010, an 8,000-ton increase from the previous year. With the help of postal employees nationwide, we're eagerly fostering a culture of conservation—and "going green" together.

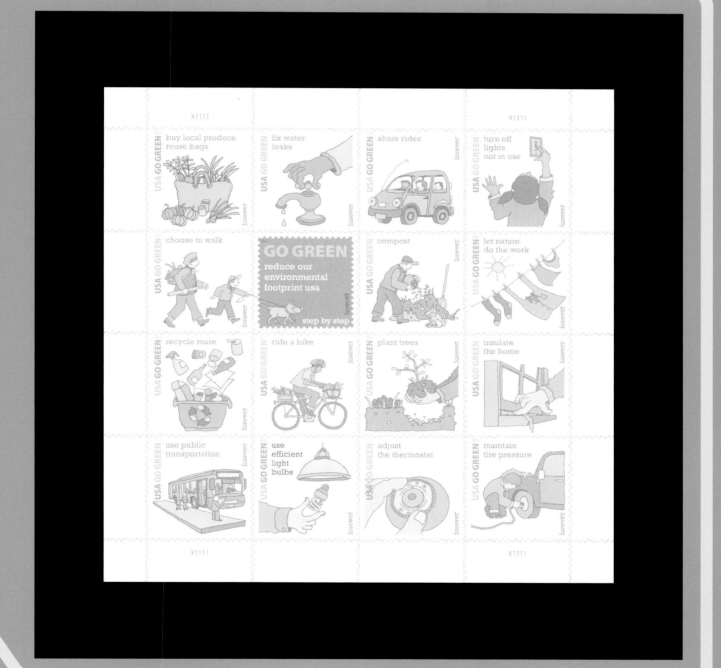

EDWARD HOPPER

B orn in Nyack, New York, Edward Hopper (1882–1967) enjoyed drawing and reading as a child. He decided early that he wanted to be an artist, but his practical parents encouraged him to focus on illustration. He unhappily did so; after a time, however, he switched to the study of fine art. One of his teachers at the New York School of Art was Robert Henri, the noted realist painter, who encouraged his students to portray all aspects of urban life.

While visiting Paris, Hopper studied the works of the Impressionists and was particularly enthralled by their use of light and pattern. He was not taken by the contemporary experiments of the Cubists, preferring instead the work of great European realist painters such as Velázquez and Goya.

While Hopper's works are primarily in the realist tradition, they are simplified and reduced in a modernist manner. Many viewers sense loneliness and an unresolved tension in Hopper's paintings. In *Nighthawks* (1942), probably his most famous work, people seated in a diner seem eerily frozen in time. *The Long Leg,* the painting featured on this tenth American Treasures stamp, allowed him to combine his love of the sea with his interest in architecture.

Interestingly, Hopper portrays an appealing scene of leisure, yet there are no people visible in the boat or on land. As with many of his paintings, a deceptively simple work reveals the extraordinary in the mundane, capturing sensations that transcend description. "If you could say it in words," Hopper once observed, "there would be no reason to paint."

LEISURE

AND LIGHT

The Long Leg is in the collection of the Huntington Library, Art Collections, and Botanical Gardens in San Marino, California. The lighthouse in this painting is Long Point Light at Provincetown, Massachusetts, and the boat is a "Knockabout" sloop, a type of craft commonly used for sailing, cruising, and fishing. The title of the painting is a sailing reference: A "leg" is one section in an alternating, zigzagging series of short and long tacks.

Like much of Hopper's work, the 1927 painting *Automat* engages the viewer with its ambiguity.

JAZZ

An innovative mélange of musical influences, jazz first flowered at the dawn of the 20th century in New Orleans, where Africans mixed with Americans, Europeans, and Caribbean islanders, giving rise to a distinctive, eclectic sound.

In New Orleans, African slaves were generally able to express themselves musically, often through rich rhythms, spontaneity and improvisation, and the use of instruments to imitate the human voice. Early jazz players emphasized group sound rather than solos, which became more important later, and tried to achieve an effect with their instruments similar to that of a single human voice, rather than the purity of tone sought by classically trained players.

Soon, traveling musicians and the newly invented phonograph disseminated jazz from New Orleans. By the early 1920s, the center of the jazz world had shifted to Chicago, as more than a million black people moved north in the "Great Migration" from the American South. So-called "Chicago

importantly, a new jazz style, bebop, left a legacy of jazz as music for serious listeners.

Bebop wasn't meant to be merely dance music; its improvised lines were faster, more insistent, and more complex. Perhaps reflecting their status as black Americans in the years before the civil rights movement, giants such as saxophonist Charlie Parker, trumpeter Dizzy Gillespie, and pianist Bud Powell transformed jazz into an outsider counterculture. They wanted to be accepted as artists, not merely entertainers.

In the wake of bebop, many factions came to dominate the scene. The intricacy of bebop married with the lyricism of earlier jazz to create cool jazz. The free jazz movement of the late 1950s and early 1960s, freed music from harmonic strictures and compositional forms, reflecting the political preoccupation with civil rights and freedom.

A mixed breed born in New Orleans, jazz has always been open to eclectic new influences. Its major figures are internationally admired—and tomorrow's legends just may come from anywhere.

jazz" is heavy in solo improvisation and made greater use of popular songs, less use of ragtime and the blues.

The next major phase was the Swing Era, when jazz reached the zenith of its commercial popularity. Swing jazz, especially as played by big bands, was characterized by tighter arrangements, a broader expressive range, and an even more pronounced separation of textures between soloists and ensemble. "Big band" music emerged mainly from New York City and focused on the interplay between orchestral sections. When bandleader Benny Goodman and his orchestra performed at Carnegie Hall in 1938, jazz moved into the nation's premier concert hall.

Several factors contributed to the end of the Swing Era after World War II. Transportation costs, musicians' wages, and hotel room prices rose steadily, making touring less practical; public taste shifted to singers such as Frank Sinatra, and then to rhythm and blues and, later, rock and roll; and the spreading popularity of television pulled audiences away from ballroom dancing. Perhaps most

2011

1959

THE PLANET MERCURY

LOCATION
Innermost planet

ORBIT
Once every 87.969 Earth days

SURFACE TEMP. RANGE
-183 °C to 427 °C

MERCURY PROJECT & MESSENGER MISSION

> HISTORY

On April 9, 1959, the names of the Project Mercury astronauts were announced to the public. In the back row stand Alan Shepard, Gus Grissom, and L. Gordon Cooper; in the front row are Wally Schirra, Deke Slayton, John Glenn, and Scott Carpenter.

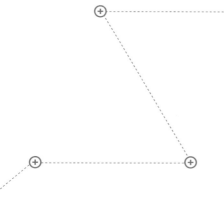

of reliability, but it was only powerful enough to achieve a suborbital flight.

As the world watched on television, Shepard blasted off from Cape Canaveral, Florida, on May 5, 1961. The flight reached a maximum speed of 5,100 miles per hour and a zenith of 116 miles above the Earth. With parachutes deploying, Freedom 7 safely splashed down in the Atlantic some 300 miles from its launch site, setting the country on a path that led to the stunning Apollo 11 moon landing in 1969.

This year, the space-minded turned their eyes from Project Mercury to the planet Mercury. Drawing its name from "MErcury Surface, Space ENvironment, GEochemistry, and Ranging," the highly anticipated MESSENGER mission will study the geologic history of Mercury; in time, it may discover tantalizing new clues to the origins of our solar system.

Launched in 2004, the MESSENGER spacecraft was successfully inserted into orbit around Mercury on March 17, 2011, and sent spectacular images back to Earth twelve days later. "The first images from orbit and the first measurements from MESSENGER's other payload instruments are only the opening trickle of the flood of new information that we can expect over the coming year," said MESSENGER Principal Investigator Sean Solomon. "The orbital exploration of the solar system's innermost planet has begun."

"It is difficult to say what is impossible, for the dream of yesterday is the hope of today and the reality of tomorrow," declared rocketry pioneer Robert Goddard, whose brilliant work helped make space flight possible. This year, two stamps celebrate historic missions that frame a remarkable 50-year period in which more than 1,500 manned and unmanned flights brought the United States closer to Goddard's "reality of tomorrow"—and to the future that awaits us in space.

Initiated in 1958, NASA's Project Mercury was the American program to send humans into orbit around the Earth. The previous year, the Soviet Union had startled the world by using an intercontinental missile to launch Sputnik, history's first artificial satellite, an achievement that marked the dawn of the space age and spurred an intense space race between the two superpowers.

In 1959, NASA selected the nation's first astronauts, screening 110 top military test pilots and ultimately choosing seven men. After nearly two years of rigorous training, Alan Shepard was chosen in a vote by his fellow astronauts to be the first American in space.

The Mercury spacecraft—Shepard's was named Freedom 7—was barely large enough to accommodate an average-sized man. The blunt end of the cone-shaped capsule was covered by a shield designed to survive the intense heat from re-entry into the atmosphere. The launch vehicle was a seven-story-tall Redstone rocket chosen for its record

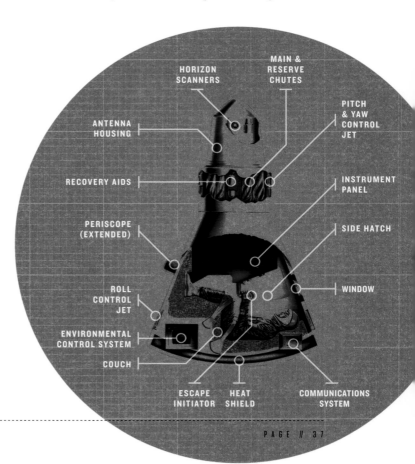

HORIZON SCANNERS

MAIN & RESERVE CHUTES

ANTENNA HOUSING

PITCH & YAW CONTROL JET

RECOVERY AIDS

INSTRUMENT PANEL

PERISCOPE (EXTENDED)

SIDE HATCH

ROLL CONTROL JET

WINDOW

ENVIRONMENTAL CONTROL SYSTEM

COUCH

ESCAPE INITIATOR   HEAT SHIELD

COMMUNICATIONS SYSTEM

"I PUT EVERYTHING I HAD INTO IT—ALL MY
FEELINGS AND EVERYTHING I'D LEARNED IN
46 YEARS OF LIVING, ABOUT FAMILY LIFE AND
FATHERS AND CHILDREN, AND MY FEELINGS
ABOUT RACIAL JUSTICE AND INEQUALITY
AND OPPORTUNITY."

— Gregory Peck, on playing Atticus Finch

GREGORY PECK

> ARTS

One of America's most respected actors, Gregory Peck (1916–2003) appeared in more than 60 films during a remarkable career that stretched from the Golden Age of Hollywood to the emergence of independent filmmaking. His intelligence, natural elegance, and searing integrity impressed critics from the start and endeared him to generations of moviegoers.

Although he played a wide variety of memorable roles throughout his career—a wayward cowboy in *Duel in the Sun* (1946), a love-struck reporter in *Roman Holiday* (1953), Captain Ahab in *Moby Dick* (1956)—Peck always grounded his performance in an innate authenticity that illuminated the screen. His thoughtful portrayal of a devoted priest in *The Keys of the Kingdom* (1944) earned him his first Academy Award nomination for Best Actor; another Oscar nomination followed for *The Yearling* (1946). In *Gentleman's Agreement* (1947), Peck played a passionate young reporter determined to expose anti-Semitism. Acclaimed by critics as well as the public, the film earned eight Academy Award nominations, including one for Peck as Best Actor. He received a fourth Oscar nomination for his portrayal of the commander of a demoralized World War II bomber squadron in *Twelve O'Clock High* (1949).

In the midst of his phenomenal rise in Hollywood, Peck remained committed to live theater. In 1947, he helped found the La Jolla Playhouse, a nonprofit professional theater company, and was an active and avid supporter for the rest of his life. Peck was President of the Academy of Motion Picture Arts and Sciences from 1967 to 1970 and also served as a longtime governor. He was an inaugural member of the National Council on the Arts and the Founding Chairman of the American Film Institute. He was National Chairman of the American Cancer Society and raised record-breaking contributions. He also devoted himself to the Motion Picture & Television Fund, which provides health care to members of the entertainment industry.

Peck's own favorite role, and the one for which he is most remembered, is Atticus Finch in *To Kill A Mockingbird*. The film earned eight Academy Award nominations, countless international honors, and the Best Actor Oscar for Peck. Perhaps Harper Lee, author of the original novel, summed it up best: "Atticus Finch gave Gregory Peck an opportunity to play himself."

A LIFE OF HONORS

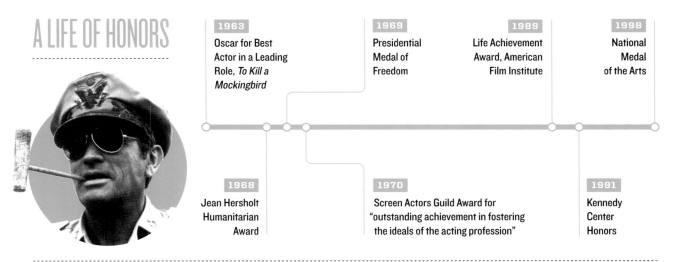

1963
Oscar for Best Actor in a Leading Role, *To Kill a Mockingbird*

1969
Presidential Medal of Freedom

1989
Life Achievement Award, American Film Institute

1998
National Medal of the Arts

1968
Jean Hersholt Humanitarian Award

1970
Screen Actors Guild Award for "outstanding achievement in fostering the ideals of the acting profession"

1991
Kennedy Center Honors

AMERICAN SCIENTISTS

MELVIN CALVIN // CHEMIST Colleagues hailed Melvin Calvin (1911–1997) as "a fearless scientist, totally unafraid to venture into new fields." He won the 1961 Nobel Prize in chemistry for tracing the workings of photosynthesis, the transformation of carbon dioxide to sugars in plants. Calvin's subsequent investigations were almost limitless in breadth and scope: He conducted research, for example, on oil-containing plants as an alternative energy source years before the worldwide understanding of this critical need.

ASA GRAY // BOTANIST Sometimes referred to as the father of American botany, Asa Gray (1810–1888) was one of the first professional botanists in the United States. He modernized the way North American plants were described and classified and made original contributions to the specialized field of plant geography. Gray was also the principal American advocate of Darwin's evolutionary theory and during the 1860s and 1870s was a persuasive proponent of the view that the theory was compatible with religious beliefs.

MARIA GOEPPERT MAYER // PHYSICIST Maria Goeppert Mayer (1906–1972) is the only woman other than Marie Curie to win the Nobel Prize in physics. During the 1940s, she developed a model for the shell-like structure of the nucleus of an atom. A team of scientists in Germany reached this same model independently, but rather than seeing each other as rivals, Mayer and Heidelberg researcher Hans D. Jensen collaborated, became friends, and co-authored the 1955 book *Elementary Theory of Nuclear Shell Structure*. They shared the Nobel Prize in 1963 for their work.

SEVERO OCHOA // BIOCHEMIST Severo Ochoa (1905–1993) has been called one of the great biochemists of the second half of the 20th century. In 1955, he became the first scientist to synthesize RNA, together with his postdoctoral student Marianne Grunberg-Manago. One year later, in the wake of his groundbreaking work, Ochoa's former student, Arthur Kornberg, synthesized DNA. In 1959, Ochoa and Kornberg shared the Nobel Prize in physiology or medicine "for their discovery of the mechanisms in the biological synthesis" of RNA and DNA.

"WHEN [THE CONSTITUTION] WAS COMPLETED ON THE 17TH OF SEPTEMBER IN 1787, I WAS NOT INCLUDED IN THAT 'WE, THE PEOPLE.' I FELT FOR MANY YEARS THAT GEORGE WASHINGTON AND ALEXANDER HAMILTON JUST LEFT ME OUT BY MISTAKE. BUT THROUGH THE PROCESS OF AMENDMENT, INTERPRETATION, AND COURT DECISION, I HAVE FINALLY BEEN INCLUDED IN 'WE, THE PEOPLE.'"

— Barbara Jordan, House Judiciary Committee speech, 1974

BARBARA JORDAN

> HISTORY

Barbara Jordan

A champion orator in high school and college, Barbara Jordan (1936–1996) was trained as a lawyer, but she found her true destiny in 1960, when she volunteered for the presidential campaign of John F. Kennedy. Jordan was initially put to work licking stamps, but after she had an opportunity to demonstrate her oratorical skills, the campaign immediately promoted her to the speaking circuit. Jordan also helped manage a highly successful voter registration program in Houston, a volunteer experience that prompted her to run for political office herself.

As a politician, Jordan held the nation's attention with her integrity, keen intelligence, and charismatic oratory. She was also a trailblazer whose prodigious list of "firsts" includes being the first African-American woman elected to the Texas legislature, the first African American elected to the Texas State Senate since 1883, and the first African-American woman elected to the U.S. Congress from the South.

In 1974, Jordan gave a moving speech about the nature of democracy during the Nixon impeachment hearings, and in 1976 she became the first woman and the first African American to deliver a keynote address to the Democratic National Convention. Her televised speech—considered the highlight of the convention—described Americans as "a people in search of a national community...attempting to fulfill our national purpose, to create and sustain a society in which all of us are equal."

During her three terms in Congress, Jordan sponsored and supported numerous pieces of legislation extending federal protection of civil rights. Afterward, she became a college professor and ethics advisor and a symbol of the potential that resides in all Americans. "Barbara's magnificent voice is silenced," observed President Bill Clinton at her funeral in 1996, "but she left the vivid air signed in her honor. Barbara, we, the people, will miss you."

GREATNESS RECOGNIZED

1984

Eleanor Roosevelt Humanities Award; inductee, Texas Women's Hall of Fame

1990

Harry S. Truman Public Service Award; inductee, National Women's Hall of Fame

1992

NAACP Spingarn Medal

1993

Nelson Mandela Award for Health and Human Rights; inductee, African-American Hall of Fame

1994

Presidential Medal of Freedom

OWNEY THE POSTAL DOG

〉 CULTURE

In the 1880s, during the height of the Railway Mail Service, clerks in the Post Office in Albany, New York, took a liking to a terrier mix named Owney. Fond of riding in postal wagons, Owney followed mailbags onto trains and soon became a good-luck charm to Railway Mail Service employees, who made him their unofficial mascot.

As Owney traveled the country, clerks affixed medals and tags to his collar to document his travels. When John Wanamaker, Postmaster General from 1889 to 1893, heard that Owney was overburdened with tags, he gave him a special harness to display them all.

In August 1895, Owney journeyed around the world, sailing out of Tacoma, Washington, on a steamer bound for Hong Kong. Upon his return during Christmas week, the *Los Angeles Times* reported that he had visited Asia, North Africa, and the Middle East. Another reporter claimed the Emperor of Japan had awarded the dog a medal bearing the Japanese coat of arms.

Upon Owney's demise in 1897, the *Washington Post* eulogized him as "one of the most famous dogs that ever lived." Mail clerks raised funds to have his body preserved, and by 1912 he was bequeathed to the Smithsonian Institution. Since 1993, the beloved canine has been on display at the National Postal Museum in a case that includes some of his medals and tags. The museum is housed in the former Washington, D.C., Post Office across the street from Union Station—both places Owney surely visited during his travels.

LUCKY PUP

Developed during the 19th century, the Railway Mail Service was an efficient and decentralized way to process mail by sorting it aboard moving trains, an innovation that became increasingly important after the Civil War. Working in the Railway Mail Service was highly dangerous; according to the National Postal Museum, more than 80 mail clerks were killed in train wrecks and more than 2,000 were injured between 1890 and 1900. However, it was said that no train ever met with trouble while Owney was aboard.

MARK TWAIN

> ARTS

Samuel Langhorne Clemens was born in Florida, Missouri, on November 30, 1835. He was still young when his family moved to nearby Hannibal, where he had a paper route and became a printer's apprentice. In 1857, he began his career as a riverboat pilot on the Mississippi, an experience that gave him the name under which he later became famous. To float safely, big steamboats needed about 12 feet of water—two fathoms, or "mark twain" in the cry of the leadsman who measured the river's depth.

When the Civil War broke out, Clemens went west and tried his luck at mining and took a job with a newspaper. In 1863, he signed an article "Mark Twain" and shot to national fame two years later with a widely reprinted comic tale known today as "The Celebrated Jumping Frog of Calaveras County."

In 1866, he sailed to the Sandwich Islands (now Hawai`i), where he filed reports for a Sacramento newspaper. Later, a cruise to Europe and the Holy Land led to *Innocents Abroad* (1869), a rousing success. *Roughing It,* about his adventures

in the West, followed in 1872. Collaborating with a neighbor, he wrote *The Gilded Age* (1873), a satiric novel about greed and corruption that gave an era its name. *The Adventures of Tom Sawyer* (1876) celebrated a mythic American boyhood; *The Prince and the Pauper* (1881) was a children's book set in Tudor England; and *Life on the Mississippi* (1883) beautifully evoked the river of his youth.

Widely considered Twain's greatest work, *Adventures of Huckleberry Finn* was published in England in 1884 and in America a year later. The novel's young narrator violates conventional morality when he refuses to betray Jim, the slave who has repeatedly shown him kindness. Huck is convinced that he will suffer eternal damnation for violating the rules he has been taught: that slavery is right and that slave-stealing is wrong. The central irony is that the rules themselves—and the status quo they support—are immoral; Huck believes he is acting immorally while doing what the reader recognizes is right.

Twain died peacefully at his Connecticut home in 1910. "All the world," one headline said, "is weeping for Mark Twain."

"THE DIFFERENCE BETWEEN THE *ALMOST*-RIGHT WORD AND THE *RIGHT* WORD IS REALLY A LARGE MATTER—IT'S THE DIFFERENCE BETWEEN THE LIGHTNING-BUG AND THE LIGHTNING."

— Mark Twain, letter dated October 15, 1888

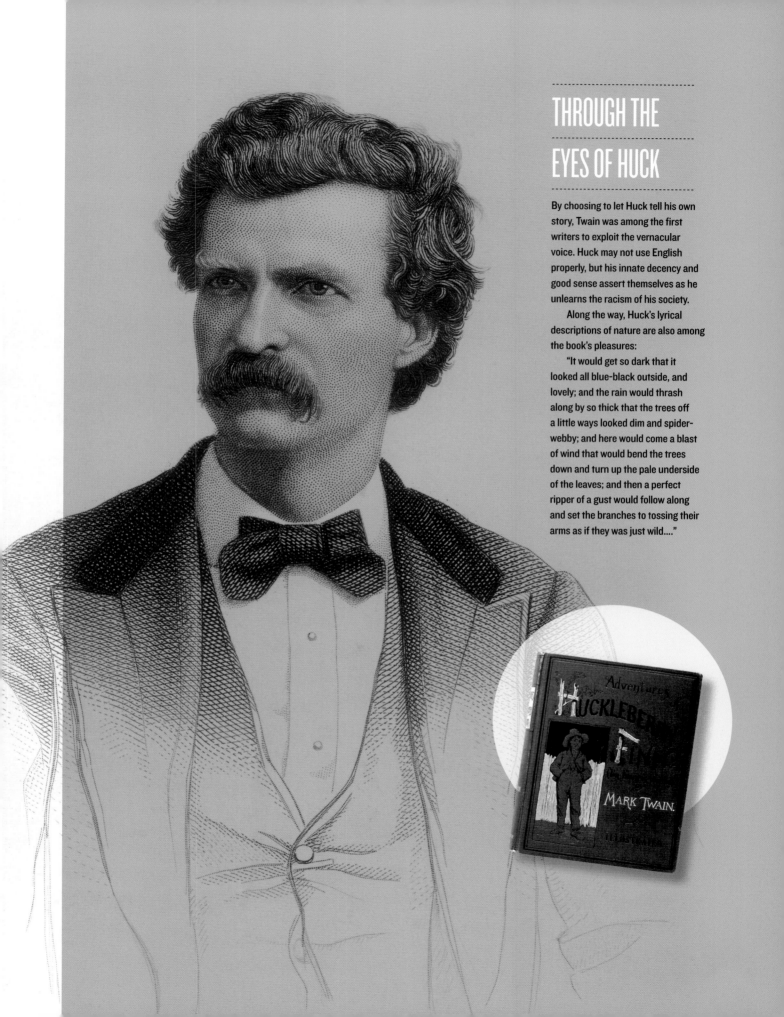

THROUGH THE EYES OF HUCK

By choosing to let Huck tell his own story, Twain was among the first writers to exploit the vernacular voice. Huck may not use English properly, but his innate decency and good sense assert themselves as he unlearns the racism of his society.

Along the way, Huck's lyrical descriptions of nature are also among the book's pleasures:

"It would get so dark that it looked all blue-black outside, and lovely; and the rain would thrash along by so thick that the trees off a little ways looked dim and spider-webby; and here would come a blast of wind that would bend the trees down and turn up the pale underside of the leaves; and then a perfect ripper of a gust would follow along and set the branches to tossing their arms as if they was just wild...."

U.S. MERCHANT MARINE

> HISTORY

Since the founding of the republic, the United States has looked to the commercial maritime industry for much of its growth and security. This issuance pays tribute to the U.S. Merchant Marine, the modern name for the maritime fleet that has long played this vital role.

In the words of maritime historian Benjamin Labaree, the clipper ship was "a unique American contribution to the glory of seafaring." Hundreds of "Yankee" clippers, noted for their streamlined shape and majestic cloud of square-rigged sails, were built from the 1840s through the 1850s. Their heyday arrived with the California Gold Rush of 1849, which hastened the need for faster sailing ships to take prospectors and supplies out West. Clipper ships eventually lost their dominance to the more dependable steamship, but during the time they "flashed their splendor around the world," as Samuel Eliot Morison has written, clippers embodied the poetry of the seas.

In the mid-19th century, steam-powered ships competed with clipper and other sailing ships for transatlantic mail and passenger service. In America, the most magnificent of these were the four large wooden-hulled, sidewheel steamships built in the 1840s by New York entrepreneur Edward K. Collins. Like many steamships of the time, they included back-up or auxiliary sailing rigs to supplement their powerful engines. Providing service between New York and Liverpool in the 1850s, they set numerous transatlantic speed records before rising costs helped bring an end to their business.

During World War I, the United States learned how to mass-produce merchant ships, while legislation in 1936 established the U.S. Maritime Commission and empowered the "U.S. Merchant Marine" to serve as a naval auxiliary unit. During World War II, the United States produced more than 2,700 Liberty ships that served in all theaters of war and sustained the Allied forces with a steady supply of food and war material. These ships were manned by members of the U.S. Merchant Marine, whose sacrifices, though less heralded than those of U.S. Navy crewmen, were no less critical to the war effort.

Without the container ship, the global economy as we know it would be impossible. Container ships were pioneered in the 1950s by Malcom McLean, a trucking operator from North Carolina. McLean's idea was to eliminate multiple handling costs by standardizing the shape of a container so that it could be easily moved between trucks, trains, and ships. Intermodal transportation took hold and transformed the global economy. By the end of the 20th century, container ships carried nearly all of the world's manufactured goods and exemplified the modern merchant marine.

PIONEERS OF AMERICAN INDUSTRIAL DESIGN

> ARTS

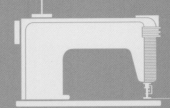

Encompassing everything from consumer goods—such as furniture, kitchen appliances, vacuums, and hair dryers—to cars, locomotives, and even airplanes, industrial design is the study and creation of products whose appearance, function, and construction have been optimized for human use. The work of these designers transformed homes and offices across the country and shaped the look of daily life in the 20th century.

Emerging as a profession in the U.S. in the 1920s, industrial design really took hold during the Depression. Faced with decreasing sales, manufacturers turned to industrial designers to give their products a modern look that would appeal to consumers. Characterized by horizontal lines and rounded, wind-resistant shapes, the new, streamlined looks differed completely from the decorative extravagance of the 1920s, evoking a sense of speed and efficiency and projecting the image of progress and affluence the public desired.

Consumer interest in modern design thrived after World War II, when machines allowed corporations to mass produce vacuums, hair dryers, toasters, and other consumer goods at low cost. Industrial designers helped lower costs further by exploiting inexpensive new materials like plastic, vinyl, chrome, aluminum, and plywood, which responded well to advances in manufacturing such as the use of molds and stamping. Affordable prices and growing prosperity nationwide helped drive popular demand.

Even as streamlining gave way to new looks in the 1960s, the groundbreaking work of industrial designers continued to transform the look of homes and offices across the country. Today, industrial design remains an integral component of American manufacturing and business and defines, in ways both large and small, the look and feel of everyday life.

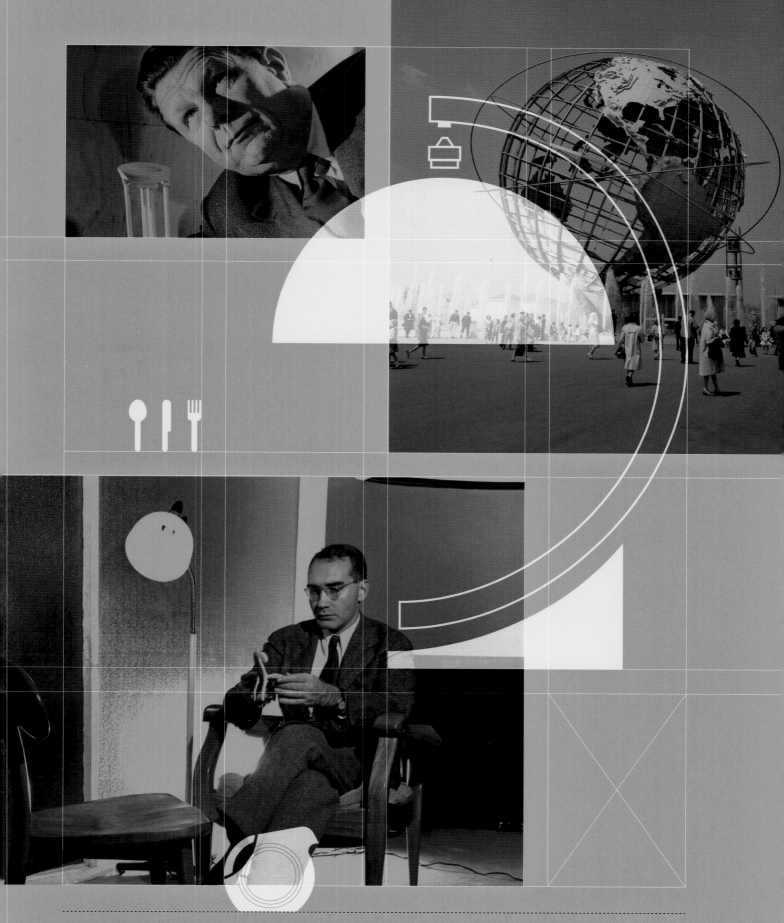

Pioneers of American Industrial Design

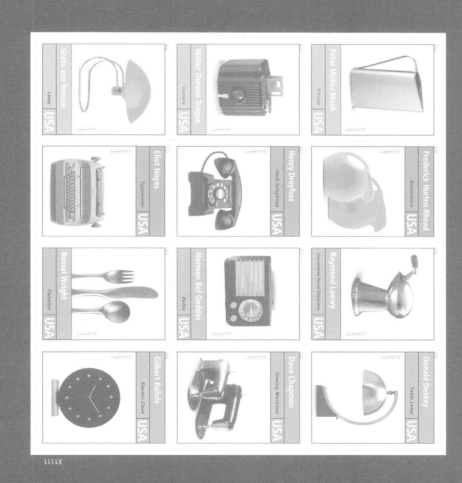

CELEBRATING LUNAR NEW YEAR:
YEAR OF THE RABBIT

Since the unveiling of the first Celebrating Lunar New Year stamp in 2008, the public has praised the series' evocative new approach to a fond, familiar subject. This vivid reimagining is the brainchild of Kam Mak, an artist who roots each new stamp in his memories of New York City's Chinatown. Mak uses his own photographs to make the sketches that become finished paintings—and beneath each stamp lie tender personal touches.

In 2001, Mak published *My Chinatown: One Year in Poems,* an acclaimed children's book that brings his memories to life by coupling his paintings with free verse. Kumquats, like those shown on this year's stamp, are eaten for luck or given as gifts, but Mak uses the fruit to remind readers that the Lunar New Year is more than just a raucous street festival:

> In Hong Kong, my grandmother
> is in her kitchen
> making pickled kumquats.
>
> In Chinatown, there are kumquats
> piled high on every street cart,
> wooden crates packed full of suns.
> Mama takes forever, hunting for
> the ones with leaves attached.
> Leaves are good luck.
>
> But she doesn't know how to pickle them.
> grandmother wouldn't tell her.
> "If I told you, you'd never come to see me again!"
> she said, and winked,
> slipping one last kumquat
> into my bowl.

For Kam Mak, the symbols that surround this ancient celebration are inseparable from family—an intimacy that shines forth in the paintings he creates.

THE YEAR OF
THE RABBIT

DATE
February 3, 2011, to January 22, 2012

FAMOUS "RABBITS"
Francis Ford Coppola, Michael Jordan,
Drew Barrymore

RABBIT HABITS
sensitive, cautious, mannerly, lucky

ROMARE BEARDEN

ne of the 20th century's most distinguished American artists, Romare Bearden (1911–1988) is celebrated for his groundbreaking approach to collage, along with his work in watercolors, oils, and other media.

In the mid-1930s, Bearden studied under the German expatriate artist George Grosz, working days as a caseworker with the New York City Department of Social Services and painting in the evenings in a rented studio in Harlem. Among his early paintings were figural works recalling his childhood roots in the South. His paintings of the 1940s were also inspired by literary sources such as the Bible, Federico Garcia Lorca's poetry, and Homer's *Iliad*.

During World War II, Bearden served three years with an all-black regiment in the U.S. Army. He was discharged in 1945 and went back to his job as a caseworker the following year. During this period, Bearden's ever-expanding study of world art ranged from the old masters and European modernism to Japanese woodblock prints and Chinese landscape painting.

In response to the civil rights movement, Bearden joined with other black artists in New York in 1963 to form the Spiral Group, which provided a forum to address issues that affected them. At one of their meetings, the idea of working collaboratively on a project was proposed. Thinking of collage, Bearden cut pictures from magazines and took them to a subsequent meeting; when no one responded to his idea, he decided to experiment on his own.

Bearden made several small collages that were then photographically enlarged. These black-and-white Projections—the name Bearden assigned to them—were exhibited in 1964 and received critical recognition. A decade later, Calvin Tomkins, art critic for the *New Yorker,* wrote: "It was as though Bearden had reinvented collage, which became in his hands the ideal medium for the transmission of all he had learned as an artist and as a man."

Bearden's multifaceted body of work also included designs for album covers, costumes, and stage sets, and has been praised for depicting the African-American experience in its full dimensionality.

"WE LOOK TOO MUCH TO MUSEUMS. THE SUN COMING UP IN THE MORNING IS ENOUGH."

— Bearden in *Ebony* magazine, November 1975

GALLERY IN MINIATURE

CONJUNCTION (1971), a collage of various fabrics with crayon and charcoal on canvas, is a large work showing a Southern social scene, reflecting Bearden's recollections of his early childhood in Mecklenburg County, North Carolina. The work celebrates the human activity of connecting through touch and conversation, and pays homage to the Southern quilt-making tradition.

ODYSSEUS: POSEIDON, THE SEA GOD—ENEMY OF ODYSSEUS (1977), a collage of various papers with foil, paint, ink, and graphite on fiberboard, is one of many images by Bearden based on literary sources. Poseidon was the archenemy of Odysseus in Homer's epic poem, *The Odyssey;* his image here combines mythic qualities with multicultural crosscurrents to suggest a larger narrative.

PREVALENCE OF RITUAL: CONJUR WOMAN, a collage of various papers with foil, ink, and graphite on cardboard, is one of a series of important collages from 1964. The power and dignity of the black woman was a central theme in Bearden's art, and the spiritual and mysterious "conjur" woman was a recurring subject. Bearden's repeated use and reinvention of motifs finds a parallel in the jazz music that influenced him.

FALLING STAR (1979) is a collage of various papers with paint, ink, and graphite on fiberboard. This image juxtaposes the ordinary, a domestic interior, with the marvelous, as seen through its windows. The falling star is a metaphor with a variety of references in art, literature, and music, and Bearden embraces these multiple meanings for the enrichment they provide to his own art.

Mail Use stamps celebrate holidays, recognize heroes, and uphold the symbols we find in our lives. Printed in large quantities to meet the varying needs of the public, they appear on cards, letters, and official correspondence, making no small impression as they pass before they eyes of millions. Irish poet William Butler Yeats may have called stamps "the silent ambassadors on national taste," but these stamps speak volumes, encapsulating America in icons, snapshots, and moments in time: the glint of a medal, the snap of a flag, or mist on the edge of a calm, endless shore.

> PART

2

MAIL USE
STAMPS

ART DIRECTOR
& DESIGNER
DERRY NOYES

ARTIST
NANCY STAHL

PLACE & DATE
OF ISSUE
**WASHINGTON, DC
SEPTEMBER 20, 2011**

SAVE VANISHING SPECIES™ SEMIPOSTAL

WITH THIS SEMIPOSTAL, Americans can contribute to conservation funds that help create hope for the future.

Proceeds from the sale of this stamp will be divided equally among the Multinational Species Conservation Funds administered by the U.S. Fish and Wildlife Service. As of 2011, these funds include the African Elephant Conservation Fund, the Asian Elephant Conservation Fund, the Great Ape Conservation Fund, the Rhinoceros and Tiger Conservation Fund, and the Marine Turtle Conservation Fund. Between 2005 and 2009, these programs distributed more than $45 million to help protect elephants from poaching, monitor sea turtle nests, create local ecotourism programs, and fund hundreds of other projects.

The cub shown on this stamp is an Amur tiger, one of five tiger subspecies. When full grown, this cat can weigh up to 650 pounds and measure 13 feet from its nose to the tip of its tail.

DISTINGUISHED AMERICANS:
OVETA CULP HOBBY

OVETA CULP HOBBY (1905–1995) led America's first female military force, the Women's Army Corps (WAC), during World War II. Attaining the rank of colonel, she succeeded in assembling a corps of 100,000 women who worked not only as file clerks and typists—jobs considered suitable for women at the time—but also as mechanics, radio operators, weather observers, intelligence analysts, parachute riggers, and heavy equipment operators.

In 1953, as the first secretary of the Department of Health, Education, and Welfare, she became the second woman to hold a Cabinet post. She began a career in journalism after marrying William Pettus Hobby, president of the *Houston Post-Dispatch* and former governor of Texas, becoming chairman of the board after her husband's death in 1964.

The stamp shows Hobby in her WAC uniform with its legendary service cap, the "Hobby hat."

ART DIRECTOR
& DESIGNER
PHIL JORDAN

ARTIST
STERLING HUNDLEY

PLACE & DATE
OF ISSUE
**HOUSTON, TX
APRIL 15, 2011**

HERBS

ART DIRECTOR
& DESIGNER
PHIL JORDAN

ARTIST
TERESA FASOLINO

PLACE & DATE
OF ISSUE
**NEW YORK, NY
APRIL 7, 2011**

SEEMINGLY LIMITLESS in the benefits they provide, herbs have long been a boon to mankind. Some herbs, such as oregano and sage, add flavor to our food, while lavender emits a light, flowery aroma that simply calms a world-weary mind. Flax, meanwhile, is often sought for its oils, which are said to have nutritional and digestive benefits, but humans have also cultivated its fibers for cloth-making for thousands of years. Foxglove, poisonous in large doses, was once seen only as an ornamental, but it is now the source of a drug that treats heart problems.

Each of the five oil paintings on these stamps depicts one of these species of herb in bloom, as well as a typical leaf and flower or seed capsule—making each stamp a lovely tribute to small plants that help us in very big ways.

LADY LIBERTY
& U.S. FLAG

FIRST ISSUED IN 2010 in a coil format, these stamps featuring American icons were reissued in 2011 in sheetlets available through stamp-dispensing ATMs.

On the first stamp, photographer Raimund Linke captures the timeless gaze of the Lady Liberty replica at the New York-New York Hotel & Casino in Las Vegas, Nevada. Half the size of the original in New York Harbor, this Lady Liberty is one of hundreds of Statue of Liberty replicas found throughout the U.S., Europe, Latin America, and Asia.

A second photograph by Ron Watts highlights the American flag, a familiar sight on definitive stamps—and, more recently, on commemoratives. The Stars and Stripes pane in 2000 highlighted the evolution of American flags over time, while the Old Glory prestige booklet in 2003 featured flag-related ephemera and American flag motifs incorporated into folk art.

ART DIRECTOR
& DESIGNER
TERRENCE W. McCAFFREY

EXISTING PHOTOS
**RAIMUND LINKE AND
RON WATTS**

PLACE & DATE
OF ISSUE
**NEW YORK, NY
APRIL 8, 2011**

LOVE:

GARDEN OF LOVE

ART DIRECTOR
& DESIGNER
DERRY NOYES

ARTIST
JOSÉ ORTEGA

PLACE & DATE
OF ISSUE
**CRESTWOOD, KY
MAY 23, 2011**

Since the first issuance in 1973, the Love series has been a source of perennial delight. Just as a garden blooms each spring, bringing forth a mosaic of life that combines familiar sights with unexpected wonders, so do the Love stamps present us with bountiful reasons to smile. While always a variation on a familiar theme, each issuance is also a pleasant surprise, as we wait to discover how our grandest human emotion has found unique and sincere new expression.

When llustrator José Ortega created the Garden of Love stamps, he began with his own love of textiles, tapestries, and mosaics—and soon found himself entwined in a delightfully abstract world of flowers, a butterfly, a strawberry, and doves, with a deep blue background evoking a bright summer day.

No newcomer to amorous themes, Ortega previously created artwork for the 2007 With Love and Kisses issuance, so these vivid symbols are near to his heart. Garden of Love, he says, "depicts the abundance of life, its generosity, whose spirit is to be shared by all its creatures. Love's definition is broader than romantic love. Love is that colorful, full feeling you get when you enjoy being a part of and sharing in the generosity of life."

This year, by using these stamps, we can express our generosity on holidays, birthdays, or any occasion when we long to affirm that the love we feel, far from evanescent, is endlessly renewable.

HOLIDAY BAUBLES

ART DIRECTOR
& DESIGNER
WILLIAM J. GICKER

ARTIST
LINDA FOUNTAIN

PLACE & DATE OF ISSUE
**NEW YORK, NY
OCTOBER 13, 2011**

THIS ASSORTMENT OF cheery stamps features four colorful ornaments that will add to the joys of the season. These festive decorations inspire fond memories of beloved baubles from childhood—objects that still have the power to enchant us today.

Drawing on colors and forms popular during the 1950s, illustrator Linda Fountain first sketched these ornaments, rendered them using cut paper, and then scanned the paper models to turn them into digital files. Fashionably "retro," the resulting stamps prove that sincere holiday wishes never fall out of fashion.

PURPLE HEART WITH RIBBON

THE PURPLE HEART is awarded in the name of the President of the United States to members of the U.S. military who have been wounded or killed in action.

The medal on this stamp belonged to 1st Lieutenant Arthur J. Rubin (1917–1978), who received it during World War II. A native of the Bronx, New York, Rubin was injured twice in July 1944 while serving with the U.S. Army near Sainteny, a village in the Normandy region of France, and was awarded a Purple Heart and an Oak Leaf Cluster to the Purple Heart. On July 8, 1944, for gallantry in action during a fierce German counterattack, he received a Silver Star. In February 1946, Rubin returned to civilian life. Upon his death, he was buried at Arlington National Cemetery with full military honors.

ART DIRECTOR
WILLIAM J. GICKER

DESIGNER
JENNIFER ARNOLD

PHOTOGRAPHER
IRA WEXLER

PLACE & DATE OF ISSUE
**SAN DIEGO, CA
MAY 5, 2011**

ART DIRECTOR
& DESIGNER
PHIL JORDAN

ARTIST
MICHAEL FLECHTNER

PLACE & DATE
OF ISSUE
**CLEVELAND, OH
MARCH 25, 2011**

NEON CELEBRATE!

MICHAEL FLECHTNER, creator of the U.S. Postal Service's first neon stamp design, honed his glass-bending skills while working in a neon sign shop after earning a Master of Fine Arts in sculpture. His educational and professional training enabled him to create neon tubing that depicted three-dimensional objects instead of the two-dimensional forms typically found in signage and other graphic neon displays.

Flechtner came up with the idea for this stamp while watching a fireworks display. "I felt that fireworks, with all their color, light, and motion was the embodiment of a celebration," he says. "Since neon is all about color and light, it was the perfect design for the medium."

PATRIOTIC QUILL AND INKWELL

AS THE MOST COMMON writing instrument at the time of America's founding, the quill pen was used in the creation of our formative documents. Such pens were typically made from goose feathers, though feathers from other birds also served the purpose.

This stamp features a digital illustration of a white quill pen dipping into a red-white-and-blue inkwell accented with stars, clearly suggesting the American flag. The inkwell and the antique writing implement combine to evoke the U.S. Constitution, the Declaration of Independence, and other documents of national significance.

ART DIRECTOR
DERRY NOYES

DESIGNER & ARTIST
CRAIG FRAZIER

PLACE & DATE
OF ISSUE
**KANSAS CITY, MO
FEBRUARY 14, 2011**

FLAGS OF OUR NATION: SET 5

"For those of us who have shared that nation's life and felt the beat of its pulse it must be considered a matter of impossibility to express the great things which that emblem embodies," said President Woodrow Wilson in his 1915 Flag Day address. This fifth set of ten Flags of Our Nation stamps captures the affection and pride we take in our flags, using icons and images where, as Wilson suggested, words so often fall short.

The Oklahoma stamp, for example, shows oil-pumping equipment, while a sailboat flying a colorful spinnaker encapsulates Rhode Island. However, many of these stamps dwell on eye-catching vistas, views of the places the flags represent. The blue flag of the Northern Marianas flies beside sandy beaches and coconut palms, while a background scene of a "low-country" marsh evokes South Carolina. On the Oregon stamp, camas lilies grow in the foreground as Mount Hood rises in the distance; milkweed plants thrive on a riverbank on the Ohio stamp.

As reminders of the living world around us, wildlife also plays a key role on these stamps. Alongside the Pennsylvania flag, a white-tailed deer pauses; half a continent away, bison roam contentedly across South Dakota. Male and female scarlet tanagers draw the eye toward the Tennessee flag, and the stamp for Puerto Rico also sports a bright little bird: the Puerto Rican tody.

ART DIRECTOR
& DESIGNER
HOWARD E. PAINE

ARTIST
TOM ENGEMAN

PLACE & DATE
OF ISSUE
COLUMBUS, OH
AUGUST 11, 2011

SCENIC AMERICAN LANDSCAPES:

VOYAGEURS NATIONAL PARK, MINNESOTA

**ART DIRECTOR
& DESIGNER
ETHEL KESSLER**

**PHOTOGRAPHER
RICHARD OLSENIUS**

**PLACE & DATE
OF ISSUE
WASHINGTON, DC
APRIL 11, 2011**

Established on April 8, 1975, Voyageurs National Park lies on the northern edge of Minnesota where the United States borders Ontario, Canada. The park was named for the voyageurs, French Canadians legendary for their canoe trips for fur trading companies in the late 18th and early 19th centuries; 55 miles of the park's northern boundary was a portion of the voyageurs' historic route. When President Richard Nixon declared Voyageurs the 36th national park, he hailed the dedicated citizens and conservation organizations who helped create it and called the park "a living legacy linking generation to generation and century to century."

The park's rock formations, many more than 2.5 billion years old, are some of the oldest exposed rock in the world. A combination of habitats supports a wealthy diversity of life, including approximately 700 species of flora, more than 240 species of birds, and 53 species of fish. Hikers and campers may hear the howl of one of several wolf packs, or watch the wolves stalk their prey across the surface of a frozen lake.

While most of the waterways at Voyageurs are frozen from mid-November until late-April, almost 250,000 people visit the park annually. Four lakes connected by waterways, more than 500 islands, a strip of mainland shore, and 26 smaller inland lakes all highlight the fact that water comprises more than one-third of the park's 218,054 acres.

Visitors to the park will find trails for hiking, cross-country skiing, and snowboarding, but as the photograph on this stamp confirms, Voyageurs is indeed a world of water. The inquisitive explorer who ventures into the park by houseboat, motorboat, canoe, or kayak will discover a realm of incredible islands and lakes—and glimpses of what traders saw when they steered their birch-bark canoes here long ago.

ART DIRECTOR
& DESIGNER
DERRY NOYES

ARTIST
DANIEL MINTER

PLACE & DATE
OF ISSUE
**NEW YORK, NY
OCTOBER 14, 2011**

HOLIDAY CELEBRATIONS:

KWANZAA

KWANZAA IS A NON-RELIGIOUS holiday that takes place each year from December 26 through January 1. The observance takes its name from the Swahili phrase for "first fruits" and celebrates seven principles based on African cultural values: unity, self-determination, collective work and responsibility, cooperative economics, purpose, creativity, and faith.

The stamp artwork focuses on a family celebrating the holiday at home, an important element of Kwanzaa. Artist Daniel Minter first carved his design into a linoleum block before scanning it into a computer for colorization. The bold colors represent the Kwanzaa flag—green for growth, red for blood, and black for the African people; these same colors are repeated in the candles that are lighted each night of the holiday.

CHRISTMAS:

MADONNA OF THE CANDELABRA BY RAPHAEL

RAFFAELLO SANZIO—the artist known to posterity as Raphael—was born in 1483 in the Italian city of Urbino, where his father taught him to paint. Drawn by the reputations of Michelangelo and Leonardo da Vinci, he went to Florence as a young man to soak up the city's learning.

In 1508, Pope Julius II summoned Raphael to Rome, where he spent the last dozen years of his short life in an inspired burst of activity. The masterpieces he produced there include the painting on this stamp, *Madonna of the Candelabra,* which dates from around 1513.

This oil-on-panel tondo, or circular painting, is now in the collection of the Walters Art Museum in Baltimore, Maryland. Art historians believe that Raphael's assistants painted some of its elements, including the angels (not shown in the stamp art) flanking the central figures.

ART DIRECTOR
& DESIGNER
RICHARD SHEAFF

PLACE & DATE
OF ISSUE
**NEW YORK, NY
OCTOBER 13, 2011**

HOLIDAY CELEBRATIONS:

EID

██████████

WHEN HE DESIGNED THIS STAMP to commemorate Eid al-Fitr and Eid al-Adha, the two major festivals in the Islamic calendar, calligrapher Mohamed Zakariya sought a new color scheme to distinguish it from the blue and gold Eid stamp that debuted in 2001. Looking to traditional Islamic manuscript art, he considered a wide range of hues crafted centuries ago from such natural sources as soils, insects, metals, and vegetable dyes.

"I designed a color for the new stamp that falls between ruby and garnet," Zakariya explains, "giving a rich, deep color that supports the gold of the calligraphy and the turquoise of the English-language text." With a reddish background color inspired by an Indian bark pigment inset with a color reminiscent of the ochre-colored turquoise stone found in China, this design evokes not only tradition, but also the craftsmanship of a fine jewel.

ART DIRECTOR
PHIL JORDAN

DESIGNER
& CALLIGRAPHER
MOHAMED ZAKARIYA

PLACE & DATE
OF ISSUE
COLUMBUS, OH
AUGUST 12, 2011

HOLIDAY CELEBRATIONS:

HANUKKAH

██████████

SPANNING EIGHT DAYS AND NIGHTS, Hanukkah commemorates the successful revolt of the Jews led by Judah Maccabee against the oppressive government of Antiochus IV and the Seleucid Empire in 165 B.C.E. Tradition relates how a miracle took place during the rededication of the Temple in Jerusalem, which had been desecrated: The remaining supply of sacramental oil, thought to be enough for only one day, burned for eight days.

On this stamp, bright colors express the joyful spirit of the holiday, and the eight shapes behind the letters spelling out 'Hanukkah' symbolize the eight days and nights of the celebration. The second "k" appears on the silhouette of a dreidel, a spinning top that children traditionally play with during Hanukkah; each letter is subtly tilted to evoke the movement of a dreidel as it twirls.

ART DIRECTOR
ETHEL KESSLER

DESIGNER
SUZANNE KLEINWAKS

PLACE & DATE
OF ISSUE
NEW YORK, NY
OCTOBER 14, 2011

ART DIRECTOR
& DESIGNER
DERRY NOYES

PLACE & DATE
OF ISSUE
**WASHINGTON, DC
APRIL 11, 2011**

GEORGE WASHINGTON BY GILBERT STUART

GILBERT STUART (1755–1828) was one of the most celebrated American painters of his era. Over the course of a long career, he created hundreds of portraits of prominent men and women; today he is best known for his portraits of George Washington.

The painting shown on the stamp is an oil-on-canvas copy Stuart made of a portrait of Washington he painted from life in 1796; that copy is now in the collection of The Sterling and Francine Clark Art Institute in Williamstown, Massachusetts. The original work, which Stuart used as a model for this and numerous other copies, is jointly owned by the Museum of Fine Arts in Boston and the Smithsonian Institution's National Portrait Gallery in Washington, D.C. It is often called the Athenaeum portrait because it was purchased and given to the Boston Athenaeum after Stuart's death.

WEDDINGS:

WEDDING ROSES

FEATURING TWO WHITE ROSES gently resting atop a piece of wedding correspondence with a white ribbon in the background, this stamp is intended for use on the RSVP envelope often enclosed with a wedding invitation and on announcements, thank-you notes, and other correspondence.

To create this stamp, photographer Renée Comet worked with art director Ethel Kessler to develop a new design that would complement the two-ounce Wedding Cake stamp originally issued in 2009. Together, these stamps will add elegant touches to wedding envelopes and help countless couples plan their most memorable day.

ART DIRECTOR
& DESIGNER
ETHEL KESSLER

PHOTOGRAPHER
RENÉE COMET

PLACE & DATE
OF ISSUE
**WASHINGTON, DC,
APRIL 21, 2011**

CREDITS

SLIPCASE

clockwise from top left: Time & Life Pictures/Getty Images & © Corbis; © Benelux/Corbis; NASA; © Leigh Vogel/Corbis

COVER

top to bottom, © Bettmann/Corbis; © Corbis; © Bettmann/Corbis; © Max Wanger/Corbis; Helen Hayes licensed by CMG Worldwide, Indianapolis, IN

RONALD REAGAN CENTENNIAL

PAGE 10 top, Getty Images; bottom, Courtesy Ronald Reagan Library
PAGE 11 © Bettmann/CORBIS

INDIANAPOLIS 500

Trademarks of Brickyard Trademarks, Inc., used under license.

PAGE 12 © Bettmann/CORBIS
PAGE 13 © Russell LaBounty/ASP Inc./Icon SMI/Corbis; inset, Courtesy Dallara Automobili

LATIN MUSIC LEGENDS

Carmen Miranda Administração & Licenciamentos Ltda
Tito Puente licensed by the Ernest Puente Trust.
Selena licensed by Q Productions, Inc., Corpus Christi, Texas
The name, image and likeness of Celia Cruz licensed by the Celia Cruz Knight Estate, Miami, Florida.

PAGE 15 background, Shutterstock Images © Sanchita; © Bettmann/CORBIS; Courtesy Estate of Celia Cruz
PAGE 16 background, Shutterstock Images © Sanchita; Photofest (2)
PAGE 17 Blanca Charloet

KANSAS STATEHOOD

PAGE 18 © Leigh Vogel/Corbis
PAGE 19 left, © Richard Cummins/Corbis; right, clipart.com

THE CIVIL WAR: 1861

PAGE 20 background, iStockphoto; top, Corbis; left, Library of Congress Map Collections; bottom, © Corbis
PAGE 21 Hulton Archive/Getty Images
PAGE 22 bottom, Time & Life Pictures/Getty Images; © Corbis

HELEN HAYES

Helen Hayes licensed by CMG Worldwide, Indianapolis, IN

PAGE 24 Photofest
PAGE 25 © Bettmann/Corbis

SEND A HELLO

Disney/Pixar Materials: © Disney•Pixar

GO GREEN

PAGE 28 top, © Max Wanger/Corbis; left, Shutterstock Images © Mike Flippo; right, © Drew Myers/Corbis
PAGE 30 top, © Tim Pannell/Corbis; bottom, Siri Stafford/Tripod/The Image Bank/Getty Images

AMERICAN TREASURES: EDWARD HOPPER

The Long Leg by Edward Hopper, is in the collection, and used by courtesy, of the Huntington Library, Art Collections, and Botanical Gardens in San Marino, California.

PAGE 32 © Francis G. Mayer/Corbis
PAGE 33 © Oscar White/Corbis

ACKNOWLEDGMENTS

These stamps and this stamp-collecting book were produced by Stamp Services, Government Relations, United States Postal Service.

PATRICK R. DONAHOE
Postmaster General, Chief Executive Officer

RONALD A. STROMAN
Deputy Postmaster General

MARIE THERESE DOMINGUEZ
Vice President, Government Relations and Public Policy

STEPHEN M. KEARNEY
Executive Director, Stamp Services

Special thanks are extended to the following individuals for their contributions to the production of this book:

UNITED STATES POSTAL SERVICE

CINDY L. TACKETT
Manager, Stamp Products and Exhibitions

CONNIE TOTTEN-OLDHAM
Manager, Stamp Development

SONJA D. EDISON
Project Manager

JOURNEY GROUP INC.

JENNIFER ARNOLD
Account Director

GREG BREEDING
Creative Director

MATT PAMER
Designer

ASHLEY WALTON
Production Designer

KRISTEN KIMMEL
Project Manager

BRAD UHL
Production Manager

PHOTOASSIST, INC.

FRANK MILLIKAN
MARY STEPHANOS
REGINA SWYGERT-SMITH
JEFF SYPECK
GREG VARNER
Editorial Consultants

MICHAEL OWENS
Image Research and Coordination

SARAH HANDWERGER
LISA JEWELL
MICHAEL OWENS
ERIN PEDERSEN
Image Rights and Licensing

GEORGE BROWN
Traffic Coordination

THE CITIZENS' STAMP ADVISORY COMMITTEE

Benjamin F. Bailar
Cary R. Brick
Donna de Varona
Jean Picker Firstenberg
Dr. Henry Louis Gates, Jr.
Dana Gioia
Sylvia Harris
Jessica Helfand
I. Michael Heyman
Janet Klug
Eric Madsen
Dr. Clara E. Rodriguez